Letters to a Young Artist in the Digital Age

Letters to a Young Artist in the Digital Age

Encouragements for a Creative Life

John Oakley McElhenney and
McElhenney, John Oakley

Press of Light and Space
Austin, Texas

Contents

A Light for Us to Forge Ahead

In 1929, Rilke's *Letters to a Young Poet* was published. Ten short letters of encouragement to a 19-year-old hopeful poet. And the master gave wonderful advice that still heartens creative artists around the world. Wonderful advice about craft, not showing your work too soon, keeping the fire alive inside even if you never get the recognition for your poetry. It is still an amazing set of letters. As if written directly to us. The spirit and ideas he expressed have kept me hopeful and energetic about my own writing.

My *Letters to a Young Artist in the Digital Age* has the same intent, to bring a new perspective to the creative process. This creative life is a path and not an end destination. Few of us will become Steven King, or George R. R. Martin, or J. K. Rowling. For those of us still on the path towards recognition or financial success, there are quite a few discouragements and barriers. It can be a struggle to keep your creative self alive and healthy.

In these letters I am in many ways writing to myself as a young aspiring writer. But I am also aware that I am writing these letters for myself as a man in his early 50s who is still seeking expression. That alone is a success story. I am still at it. I am still writing, singing, and playing music as if I were still in the race. But of course, it's not a race, it is life. And if you are a creative person, you have a long life ahead. And if you are lucky, and perseverant, you will continue to create well into your old age.

And in many ways I am writing these letters to my future self as well. Encouraging my current, early 50s self to keep writing. I have the magic perspective of time travel to bring all three of these "artists" together in my mind, as I write the little ideas for keeping creativity as a main goal of life. This is my goal: if there is anything I can do to help others find their path, let me share my own experience.

So, let's start there. This is my experience, in my years of being an artist. I have had some successes and many failures, but I've always gotten back up, brushed myself off, and continued with the work. Along this path I have come up with some ideas that help me maintain my hope, my energy, and my focus as an artist. I am writing these pages to you if you are on the same journey. What we need are friends along the path to cheer us on. These letters are my cheering you on. And in many ways, I am cheering myself on, as I continue to create and believe that my life's gift is in this creating.

I hope you find creativity in your life. And if I can be of any help to you, let me know. I am over here in my own tunnel of life, furiously creating myself, and I will share what I can of the light for us to forge ahead.

This book is dedicated to my niece, nephew, and my two creative children.

1

Your Personal Creative Cloud

If you have creative ambitions (writing, visual arts, music), you have a hard road ahead. About 1% of creative artists make a living off their art. I know there are plenty of exceptions. And I know that number is low. But I'm thinking of a living that doesn't require scrambling each month to make rent. I'm talking about a living that provides for a family, with a mortgage and health insurance. If that's the "life" you are thinking of, you need a day job. You need to CREATE. But you also need a way to make a living while the world takes its sweet time learning who you are and appreciating your wonderful works of art.

Here are a few things about writing that I've learned or read:

- Writers want to be read (viewers online, ebook or book sales).

- Writers want to be appreciated (comments online, book reviews, blog comments).

- Writers need to focus more on the writing than the immediate gratification that comes from soliciting the little appreciations.

- Any writing on Facebook or for non-essential purposes is just wasted energy for a writer.

- Dissipating your energy on Facebook or fishing for compliments does not serve your writing, it releases some of the pressure we feel to complete something. By letting off some of that pressure, we can get complacent.

Rilke, in his *Letters to a Young Poet*, said it better than anyone before him. (And I'll paraphrase from memory rather than quoting.)

- Write because you love it so much that you would die if you didn't write.

- Don't look for others to validate your writing.

- Your writing is for you and your enjoyment.

- Don't share your work unless it is truly finished.

- Don't worry about becoming a poet, just write poetry.

- If you write, you will improve.

- That is enough for the poet, to write. Asking to be appreciated is a trap that will kill your inspiration.

- Inspiration is nice, but writing every day is the hard work that is required to be a writer.

- You already ARE a poet (writer). By writing, you are a writer.

- Write because you can't stop writing.

Eventually, if your writing gets exceptional, the praise and accolades may come. They probably won't, but that should not discourage you.

Writing is a very lonely task. You can't write while carrying on a conversation with others. Often people in relationships with writers tend to feel abandoned. It requires long stretches of time, alone. And today, a writer who makes a living from his or her writing is very rare. Sure, you could make a couple thousand dollars on your own, if you are very successful at self-publishing, and perhaps $15,000 if you sign with a publisher and have a hit. But neither of those options will put food on the table. And if you have a family, or want to have a family, you might think up your Plan B, if you don't break the Stephen King code of success.

It's okay. Write anyway. Poetry never pays. Prose is read only by a small group of people. But that doesn't mean you have to focus on business titles or technical manuals. It does mean that if you declare yourself a poet, you're going to need a day job as well. Let poetry and prose be your night job. If you sputter out and give it up, that's okay. Give yourself a break. Relax. If the writing is within you, it will come back stronger and with more intention. Nothing proves a writer like a full-time job and a family and THEN WRITING.

No one is going to welcome you to the successful writing adventure. Because very few have tasted it. And some of them are defensive and worry that your book might take sales or exposure away from their book. It's not true. Any gift you give another writer, in praise and encouragement, comes back to you within yourself. You see, we're writing because we can't not write. We write poetry because we have to. If the poetry stopped, so would our poetic hearts.

Be poetic if that's your bent. Be a journalist if you prefer. And make sure you have your day job figured out, because nothing kills a writer quicker than unpaid bills and lack of food and shelter.

Write. Yes.

But do your work first.

2

Pointing Your Arrow: The Artist's Way to Happiness

It's not the success I've had that gives me joy. It's not fame or fortune that pleases my soul. For me, it's the perfectly struck chord, the phrase that captures exactly what I'm feeling, the letters scattered across a handwritten notebook that please ME. That's the important part to remember. It is your heart that is listening. It is your heart that is the most important audience. If you love your craft, your fame and acceptance will be less important to your happiness.

So what is the goal of this creative life? What do I get from being bombarded daily with poetic ideas, song fragments, and aspirations towards becoming an artist? If I am continuing to "point" my arrow, as in, sharpen my craft, to what end am I laboring? And if I continue to strive, write, sing, create, what is my goal? What am I aiming my pointed arrow at? Where am I pointing this creative life of mine?

I'm in my 50s. I've already lived 12 years longer than John Lennon. And if you watch any of the documentaries of his life, can you imagine a more successful creative life? And yet even at the height of his fame, he was still searching, still stretching to express himself artistically. With all of the wealth of the world, what he wanted the most was time with his family. He missed Julian, but when Sean was born, John basically took to becoming a stay-at-home dad. His joy was his family. And even as his life was cut very short, remember that point. One of the most successful creative spirits on the planet was still seeking more time with his family. Time and experience that could never be regained. Ask Julian Lennon about the loss of a famous father.

So even in achieving the greatest fame and appreciation possible, John Lennon was struggling to find more time to be with his family.

What is the goal of trying to express ourselves creatively? If fame seems elusive, are there other reasons to listen so intently, to strive daily to write, paint, craft? For me, the experience of living my life through the lens of art is part of my personal life mission. It sounds woo woo, I know, but here's what I'm saying.

- I listen a bit more deeply to myself in trying to understand and express my feelings.

- I listen to others and record experiences in my mind with a fine attention to detail, in order to absorb as much of the essence as possible. Sometimes the level of detail makes recalling experiences a bit more vivid.

- I am tuned in rather than tuned out. I don't watch much television or read much mass media. I am actively trying to create my own story. I am weaving my own tapestry of experience into a tale of song, poetry, image, and story.

- I get great joy from my own work. A poem well turned is a thing that can make my whole day. It gives *me* great pleasure. If I'm happy, well, that's a pretty good result.

- After capturing a story or an idea, I can let it go more fully. Once I've written about an experience (good or bad), I begin to understand it more fully. In the case of hard experiences (losing my father or my older sister, for example), my artistic expression helps me process the grief. By telling the story, I get a chance to re-experience any event in my life and thus reprocess the feelings associated with it.

The art in itself is a joy and a comfort. The act of creation is a form of prayer. When I am deep in my creative process, I am also in the flow. The flow is like meditation. My troubles and personal frustrations are forgotten while I am in flow.

What's the goal of my art?

My goal is to live life as fully as I can. To enjoy the time I have with my kids and to make a living. So I have not been able to make the two aspects of my life combine into a famous artist path, that's okay. It's not the idea of becoming famous that drives me, it's the joy that the act of creation brings me today. And if I can write a new song while my kids are busily going about their day in and around me, what could be more joyful?

Aim at your own heart.

Then, regardless of your fame or fortune, you are at least making one person happy. And often, if that happiness is genuine, the art will also touch others with a happy resonance. You can hear the joy in John Lennon's songs about Sean. He was hitting his stride again as a solo artist just as he was cut down by a mad man. And in many ways, he was a victim of his own fame. And yet his legacy and music lives on.

3

Perseverance and Habit: This Creative Morning

Do you love the work? Is it life and breath to you?

The creative craft is about perseverance. Staying with it. There is no American Idol of creative process, there is no short cut.

Very few people get to be Taylor Swift. The rest of us must make due with the mundane life AND the creative life in parallel. While we are working at our craft, we are also working at making a living. If you can find the way to do both with the same work, you are lucky. And perhaps unlucky, too. Beware the paid working gig that saps your creative juice. Many a copywriter has never surfaced from the pithy and promotional.

So what does it take to fall in love with your work?

Time at craft is probably my most important motivator. If I am writing, or playing music, then I am in the groove. When I am away from the craft for any extended period of time (writing or music, in my case), there is some internal resistance to getting back in there and getting back to work. It's as if the studio becomes a hostile environment. Or that anything other than doing the work has become preferable. An afternoon wandering around a book store might feel inspirational, but it can also be avoidance. The best remedy for avoidance is to jump back in. Face the chair, the empty page, the "record on" button.

Being in the process of creation is the antidote to ennui. Resistance can be boredom. Or fear.

How do you fight the blahs?

Habit: Starting a habit is great if you can get there. Finding my quiet space took 40+ years. Perhaps you can find yours earlier in your career. For me, the morning hours are sacred. No one else is awake. I brew my cup of coffee and crack open the laptop for a session. Some mornings I know exactly what I will work on, some mornings the inspiration actually pulls me out of bed an hour earlier. It's as if my spirit anticipates this pre-dawn release. Finding this quiet time and making a habit of rising when I wake up and simply writing was a process.

The morning pages of Julia Cameron's *The Artist's Way* (http://juliacameronlive.com/basic-tools/morning-pages/) are a great technique to cultivate this inner drive and dialogue towards your creative dreams. And in the habit of writing and aspiring towards something bigger than yourself, you'll find your mind wakes up ready to go, ready to create.

Today, writing is easier for me to jump into in the morning. The process is about creation; the medium you choose is less important. It can start with writing your morning pages and progress to writing or painting or composing. The habit is the thing. Your spirit will begin to crave the expression time. And the momentum grows the more you practice this creative grooving. This habit has formed the heart of my creative craft. I am never at a lack for time to create. No one is waiting for me at 5:30 or 6:00 a.m. Only me and my imagination.

Structure of ideas: Another part of my momentum-building process is creating structures. If you can design containers for your music, or paintings, or writing, you can pour your ideas into the containers. These "structures" have an energy of their own.

When I came up with the idea of doing these letters, for example, I had a quick win with the first six letters. I didn't have to work at coming up with the next letter each morning. I was on a roll. The structure, and idea, of creating a series of inspirational, how-do-you-do-it letters was enough to pull the first six ideas out of me, almost without effort. And then I got distracted or decided to take a break. I was not trying to complete a book of letters overnight. I almost felt the process was too easy. Perhaps I was creating something of vanity rather than something of value. But I had to let that idea drop in the trashcan. There is no place for doubt when you are building your structure or your habit. Doubt is the killer.

No, I did not doubt the process when it came easy. And I don't think I lost inspiration when I turned my writing back towards other things. I have a confidence in the process, in the writing, and was not worried about losing the energy for completing these letters. I had the same sense that giving the next letters a bit of time to percolate was a good idea. Because I have found a way to capture and retrieve well, I am not concerned with losing the thread.

Capture and retrieve: Finally, developing a good capture system for your various ideas is a key ingredient for perseverance.

At the moment, I am committed to keeping my focus on the livelihood branch of my creative life. I need a more stable income stream to support my family and the things I want to accomplish in the next period of my life. And with this commitment I am using my drive towards music as a reward. (I'm wondering if this is some type of avoidance? I'd hate to think I'm losing the ideas, rather than storing them away.)

My internal commitment is this: until I find the next client engagement (which requires focus, energy, and dedicated time and action, to find it), I will not jump off into any large musical projects.

But it's the capture system that has me confident that I am not losing any of the ideas that are still coming along. If you can capture the essence of an idea into a system that you will not lose, you may be able to return to the inspiration and build up the full idea. In music, this can be a vocal idea, a guitar progression, or just a piece of music that is particularly inspiring. In my toolkit I have several processes for capturing my ideas.

My iPhone video makes a great capture tool for musical ideas. I can turn the camera on myself and my guitar and essentially show myself the idea on video. I can call out the tuning, if it's non-standard, and then proceed to show myself the progression. In this way I can get an idea down in a matter of minutes, rather than spend half a day recording the rough tracks. The idea is that this seed will be enough to pick the song idea back up when I have the half-day to devote to it.

The problem is retrieval. I have about six of these ideas in various formats in various locations of my digital life. I need to get the three ideas off my phone and put them in a folder on my laptop so I can get back to them, even if my phone is stolen. I will do that directly after finishing this piece this morning. Once I have the "idea" captured, I can move back to the activities that require priority processing. I'll be back in the musical fold, but I know it takes a much larger commitment of time, so I will delay the gratification on these ideas. So far, the momentum has been easy for me to pick back up from these video snippets.

Find your simple capture system for when the ideas come at inconvenient times. Then make sure you can rekindle the spirit from your capture and that you can catalogue them and find them later, when you're in need of inspiration.

The keys to perseverance:

Habit.

Structure.

Capture and retrieval.

4

Opening to the Poetic in Your Life: Poetic Listening

Poetry is about listening. To your heart. To the words streaming around you. The hardest part is to let go and be poetic. Take all ideas of form, shape, and poetry that you learned and toss them out. Stop thinking about it and put a Word. On. A. Page.

One word or image is all it takes to set your mind in a spiral. You can choose to listen and record, or you can ignore the impulse towards beauty or sadness. I guess that's some of the resistance. Poetry is feeling. If you're avoiding feeling things, perhaps it's hard to drop down into the listening mode required to hear the poetic in your life. But if you are shutting out the sadness, in many ways, you are shutting out the happiness as well.

Flights of fancy are always poetic. Love, or the rush of love, is poetic. You feel little nuances all the time. The goal is to tune-in your radio set just a bit more accurately. If you are flooded with stress, activity, inputs (TV, email, Facebook), you may have a harder time hearing the beauty around you. And the sadness is around you, too.

We are poetic beings. A good percentage of our thoughts is language-based. Words are coursing through you every second, and you are filtering them in a very controlled (subconscious) way. The idea is to tune into the stream just a bit more and listen *through* the filters to some of the emotional language rushing by. We are trained to filter this "emotional" stuff out. I mean, if we were fully feeling everything, we'd collapse at every mention of global injustice, local tragedy, or personal regret. We've got to filter out a lot of emotional language in the course of living productive lives.

As you become a bit more conscious of the poetic language that's coursing through you, try grabbing a few images, or words, here and there. Put them down. Laugh. Throw the poem away.

Poetry is not about success or failure, it's about listening. It's about exploring your own experience of life. It's about tuning into your lifestream and plucking out the emotional bits so you can celebrate *your* human experience. There is no successful poem. There is only resonance or not. The resonance you are looking for is what happens inside of you when you hit a phrase, an expression, a word, that makes you feel that *ah-ha!*

If you feel it, chances are you've captured a slice of the loving/failing/falling human experience. And if you can capture something honest and pure, you don't have to wonder if it's good. If you got it, you'll feel it.

Then you have to let it go.

So much of what represses our poetic impulses is the evaluation and judging of what we've written or created. You want to cut out that need for success, that judging of good or bad. What you want to hear, look for, experience, is the feeling of a YES when you capture a moment. If a poem has a big YES for you, that is enough.

Sharing poetry is another story. Some people will never get it. Some people cannot hear you. And some will simply not resonate with what you've captured. You're best off keeping most of your poetic meanderings to yourself. When the poetic storm has become strong in your life, the poems will burst out, and at some point you will no longer be able to contain them. At this point, when the coursing rage of language and abstract catch-and-release process is strong within your life, then... you can share if you know your creative process is not at risk or under review.

A poem either resonates with someone or it doesn't. It's like the book you try to read that feels flat in your 20s but lights up in your 40s. If one person lights up in response to one of your poems, you might begin to get a little heady, a little high. I caution you to reflect back to your own experience and your own process. The biggest trap in creative process is to find something successful and then try to repeat it.

Dip your hand in the flowing/coursing of yourself. Pull up an idea, image, or sound to share. And move along. Don't fancy yourself a poet.

Imagine this awkward scene at a party.

> *You're meeting some people for the first time. "Hi, John, what do you do in the real world?"*
>
> *"I'm a poet."*
>
> *Imagine the feeling you might get hearing someone claim that title. What's your first response? "Oh cool. What have you written?"*
>
> *The only really killer response at that point, the only response that's going to win love, money, and fame is to say, "Well, I've just been chosen as the poet laureate of the United States."*

We are all a long way from there, right?

Poetry is very personal and precious. Don't let your self-expression be squelched by others' opinions or reviews. Do your poetry. If it pleases you, be joyous with that. If it pleases someone else, you've just had an answered prayer.

You can imagine that e. e. cummings had a lot of "what?" responses to his poems. Fortunately he kept going.

the
      sky
            was
can dy lu
minous
            edible
spry
        pinks shy
lemons
greens   coo   l choc
olate
s.

  un   der,
  a   lo
co
mo
      tive   s   pout
                        ing
                              vi
                              o
                              lets

Just keep going.

5

Paralyzed by Opportunity: The Firehose of Ideas

It's not ideas that count, it is the execution of those ideas.

Every day of your life, as a creative person, you are going to be assailed by your mind with 227 ideas. (There's no rhyme or reason for this number; yours is likely to be much higher.) The challenge as an artist is how to capture and filter all the incoming ideas and make sense of them. Your life's work depends on the projects you pick and the projects you leave behind. But first we have to deal with the firehose.

I am a victim of this malady, even in my 50s. My ideas come much faster than I can keep track of them. Remembering that they are merely ideas, I can bat a number of them back into my subconscious without much effort. These are the big ideas, the huge ideas, ideas that I will be working on for years.

A rock opera and stage performance, for example. Or one of four screenplays that are haunting my creative imagination and are in various stages of being written.

But it's the flow of ideas that's the issue. How to make sense, set priorities, and filter out the noise.

FIRST: Your capture system

How do you make note of the rush of ideas so that you can evaluate and revisit them later? If you don't have a capture system, you can't flush the idea out of your available memory space to make room for new ideas. The little idea (about a color to use in a new painting, for example) will swirl around in your mind, taking up endless cycles of your processing power, while you try to "not forget" and yet "not pay attention" to this little idea. The key is getting the idea down in a form you can recover easily. The better your capture system, the easier it is for you to push the rush of ideas into LATER (painting), LATER (writing), LATER (music) categories for mulling over and processing later.

Your capture system is only as good as the confidence you have in your ability to re-find and recall the energy that was expressed in the idea. As you get better at capturing, your mind will get better at letting go and freeing up space for other ideas or (for many of us) the work you have to do for a living. Your creative life will permeate your working life if you let it. And this is a good thing. Until it's overwhelming your work life. When you begin calling in sick because you stayed up all night working on a piece, you'd better think about the choices… (Sorry, I'm not trying to be your parent, just a friend along the artist's path.)

SECOND: The filtering process

When the firehose of ideas is fully open, you will be interrupted frequently by flights of creative fancy. The first step is to remember ideas are just ideas; it's the execution of the ideas that makes you an artist. The second step is to know when the idea is valuable and needs to be captured, or if the idea is more like a feeling. When your inspiration is a specific detail about a project you are engaged in, the capture should be fairly simple. (Do this-this-and-this next time you open the song file.) When your idea is more meta (or not connected directly to any action, but more of the grand idea variety), you can often toss it back into the supra-consciousness knowing that your big ideas require thousands of inspirations, and often it's the gestation of a meta–idea that will become the framework for future projects. These too are easy to jettison out of our real-time memory with the confidence that they will return in more evolved ways later.

Then there are the ideas that are fleeting and hard to capture, hard to nail down, more inspiration and feeling than detail. And these are the ones you need to pay attention to. Entire song compositions can happen for me in the first five minutes after I wake up in the morning. If I don't pay attention, those gifts are gone. And it's often not convenient for me to immediately turn on the recording studio and spend the next 30 minutes trying to capture the essence. You may have similar epiphanies upon waking or in the moments just before you fall asleep. At this point, you have a decision to make. If this "movement" is worth capturing, how can I do it and still maintain my obligations for the day? (Getting my kids to school on time, for example.)

THIRD: Radical capture of ideas

This one takes some creativity. And depending on your medium, you can create your own unique ways of getting at the heart of the idea without actually having to execute the entire idea in that very moment, which in this case is not feasible.

I'm going to take this idea and parse it into my personal methods based on the creative medium that's being activated. For me that's music, expository writing, poetry, or visual art.

Radical music capture

1. Leave yourself a voice mail. Just sing the idea into your voice mail. If you're traveling, on a bus, or walking down the street on the way to work, don't miss the little idea that hits you. Call yourself on the phone (or use a recording app on your phone) and leave a message. With music, my melodic ideas are short and simple. But later they can be unpackaged into full songs.
2. Use your phone to video your guitar or piano playing.

Since I'm not all that versed in writing down my musical ideas, I turn on my selfie camera in video mode and record myself playing the guitar pattern. If the guitar has an odd tuning, I can spell that out at the beginning of the video.

3. Play it into Garageband, or some other quick/simple tool for recording. Sometimes I want a tempo track or a second part. I can fire up Garageband (Mac) from anywhere (heck I think it's on my iPad too) and grab a few measures of my idea using the internal Mac microphone. Or I can use Garageband to give me a simple tempo or drum pattern and then use my phone to video capture the guitar.

Radical writing capture

1. Evernote is your friend. Since the little app Evernote exists in the cloud, it's always available on your phone, your computer, or your tablet. The notes you make on one device are synced to all the devices. YAY.

2. Remember the outlining technique you learned in school? Outlines rock for getting the structure of a writing piece down before you ever write it. If you can do the outline in three minutes and get on with your day, because you have other things that simply have to be done first, go for it. You can write from your outline when you have the time.

3. Poetry. Yes, this isn't really a capture device as a radical way to store verbal information in a short period of

time. Often when I'm writing a longer piece about some emotional topic, I will also write the same story in a poem. If I can get the essence (for me) down in a poem, the I can return to write the larger piece later. And there's a lot of crossover between poetry and music… so there's that.

4. Text Editors are your friend. No formatting, just text. Save with a descriptive name and recall it later. (Microsoft Word is a hog and takes a while to load.)

Radical visual art capture

1. Sketch. I can design 10 website ideas in three minutes with a pen and piece of paper. Get good with your hand skills. Draw out the idea for execution later.

2. Quick Capture with PowerPoint or other image-driven app. Some of my bigger ideas are better facilitated by a graphic program. And when at my corporate job, occasionally all I had was PowerPoint. So I got really good at sketching out ideas in PowerPoint. Sure, they were not even close to the finished form that I wanted, but the idea was captured, and I could let it go, knowing that I could return to my actual canvas or drawing pad later to fully realize the idea.

3. Take a picture or screen grab of what you were looking at when the inspiration came to you. A lot of artistic work is derivative, don't be ashamed of that. We're all "standing on the shoulders of giants."

You've got to listen and tune into the rush of ideas, but you cannot let them overwhelm you. This is a hard trick. The pull is strong, for me, to drop into musician mode and ignore all the other modes that are required of me (dad, worker, boyfriend). But I can use various capture and filter techniques to grab the incoming ideas and put them in my capture system. Later I can map out a plan for them to become works of art or just one of the 227 ideas that shot through me today.

Just keep going.

6

Focus Yourself: Cutting Away the Distractions

Not everything is a distraction. You cannot create 24/7. Things like sleep, play, exercise, love, and daydreaming are essential elements to finding your balance in life. And work, if it is not your art, can be a massive, but necessary, distraction that will keep you away from your real vocation. Seek out distractions like mind clutter and eliminate as many of them as you can. This is why late late nights and early mornings may be your best times for creative production, as there are far fewer distractions.

But distractions are not the only enemy of your creative talent. Maybe the more important discussion is not distraction but focus. Focus is your superpower for killing distractions and getting on with your creative work.

How do you create focus in your art?

One way I have found to build creative momentum and give focus to my production is to imagine the series or sequence of work that becomes fascinating to me. Note it is you in need of the structure. If you can fascinate yourself with an idea (one self-portrait a week, one song a day), you may find a process that pulls you along, that finds illumination of some deep creative recess in your brain, and you will begin working the idea like a prayer, ceaselessly dreaming up new approaches or chapters of the project.

Before you can capture the imagination of others with your brilliance, you've got to fascinate yourself. In the fascination you may be able to find the momentum to carry you along. As you have successes in your process and continue to find joy in the craft of building this larger body of work, you will be refining your craft. Really, that's the goal, at this stage in your life. Sure, you are creating a body of work, but as a young artist you are really trying to find the niche that gets you super-conducted as an artist. Only through this super-conductiveness, this faster and faster acceleration of your art, can you build up to the super-collider of joy that will become your life's work.

Of course, you realize, I'm speaking more from theory than practice here. At least in terms of finding the path to achieve escape velocity. In my 50s, I am still working for a living. I am still looking for the super-conductive path that could pull me off the planet and into orbit. But I'm not complaining. At this point, distraction is less and less of a problem for me.

Here are a few of the distractions that I have eliminated.

- TV: I might watch a show (Game of Thrones, Mad Men, Orange Is the New Black), but I don't turn on the TV, ever. I don't even have one.

- News: TV news might be the worst for me, because I cannot get the visual images out of my brain, but even newspaper, newsfeeds, Huffington Post are all distractions.

- Partying: Some is good, too much is a dead end.

- Driving my body to exhaustion: Yes, in the name of art it is all too possible to let inspiration destroy our energy by going too far.

- Games: I love a good game as much as anyone, but they will suck you in and suck out some of the most valuable hours of the day.

- Desserts: Too much dessert and I wind up fat and tired.

- Reading, listening, exploring: These are wonderful and essential things in moderation, but they can also be a distraction.

Find your distractions. Learn which ones feed you and charge your energy back up. And eliminate or limit the ones that pull your spirits and motivations down.

Today, you still have most of your life ahead of you. But the sooner you discover your energies and contain your passions by capturing the excess energy in your creative process, the further along the path you will be by the time you reach my age.

The part of the process that is essential to understand: this is a marathon that you are running for the rest of your life. If you sprint around the track to win in your 20s, you may wear out or burn out too soon. Find the glowing ember in your mind that you can count on during times of highs and lows. Find the project that consistently pulls your energy and focus back. Give yourself ceaselessly to your art. Make this project your mistress. Make love to your canvas, or guitar, or word processor. The successes of life and love will follow in the long race. But your pace, stride, and cadence are more important to establish at this point in your life.

I am still working on my training. I am still striving to eliminate the distractions from my life. And, of course, I am still seeking the trajectory that will take me up and out of the world of non-creative work. The cool thing is, I'm still a believer. I am still arcing towards my creative projects. I am still trying to erect creative structures I can lean into with my imagination.

To pull back from distractions is to pull up on the controls of your art and aim skyward.

If you can find the key to your motivation and commitment,

you have unlocked the third rail, the one with the electric power to turn up the speed on your own bullet train.

7

Stop Talking: Do the Work, Don't Talk About Doing it

If you're talking about your work rather than doing it, you are letting out a lot of energy. This energy (joy, excitement, recognition, community, support) is better used by focusing on doing the work rather than talking about doing the work. It's an easy concept, but it's harder to learn and master.

When you are cranked up about a project, it is hard not to share it with others. Yet, the minute you learn how much power comes from not sharing it but rather working to finish it, the quicker you will get the amazing benefit from this idea of containment. You want to contain and build the energy in your creative work and use it exclusively for actually doing the work, rather than explaining it, or celebrating it, while it is still incomplete.

Have you ever been totally jazzed about a piece of work you are in the middle of, and you want to tell everyone? Or you have a specific friend who is a supporter or an artist as well, and you love spending time brainstorming and venting about your work with each other. Stop that. The celebration is for after the publication or show or performance.

By talking about your idea, you might think you are giving voice or fleshing it out. But you are actually trying to get a bit of the recognition for your great work. Even in the most supportive environments, with the most supportive artist friends, every word you say about your work is 100 words you are losing in the progress of the work. (Apply as a metaphor to any creative discipline you like.)

Why are you talking about it rather than doing it?

- You want support (what's hard about being an artist?).
- You want accolades (we all want to be recognized for our art).
- You want to brainstorm.
- You want to let off some steam from the hard day.
- You want to join in the "high" of doing great work.
- It's natural to want to share things that are making you excited.
- You want to be loved.

All of those things are part of the artist's struggle. Like the common internal question, "Why am I working so hard at this if I'm never going to be recognized or, better yet, paid for my work?" If you are an artist, you are probably struggling with some of these identity and livelihood issue right now. That's part of the path of the artist.

Part of the magic of *The Artist's Way* by Julia Cameron is the morning pages. Briefly, the idea is to wake up in the morning and start writing. Your goal is stream of consciousness and volume or time writing. You set a timer and begin. Whatever comes, you write. Without thinking too much about it, you simply stroke the pages until your time is up.

What this process unlocks is your internal collaborator and cheerleader. The "pages" begin to form a relationship between your consciousness (the writing) and your subconsciousness (the flow of ideas). As you get more familiar with this connection, the stream of consciousness becomes more fluid, easier, quicker. And when you really get going, you're anticipating the morning pages with excitement. It's a bit like talking to a friend, except in this instance there is little or no loss of energy. In fact, your artist's voice may become stronger as your subconscious thoughts gain more voice in your life. As you listen to the crazy and exciting things your mind is rambling on about, you may begin to see patterns, evoke ideas, or change the direction of your creative path.

And the morning pages can get scary for some people. When the weird and frightening ideas pop out of your unfiltered mind onto the page, it's a jarring experience. But this is some of the reason we become artists. We need to connect with this sublingual idea machine and give language and voice to the ideas that begin percolating. It's like self-hypnosis, or self-analysis in the Freudian way, and you simply answer the questions: "Then what happened?" "How did that make you feel?" "Can you tell me more?"

In this way, you begin calling out your strange ideas. You begin cultivating a dialogue with some of the swirling beasts that might have been swimming around in your mind for years and years. Our creative process is like saddling them up and riding them onto the canvas or into a song. The morning pages process can unlock a huge amount of energy and set you on a path towards a more creative life.

But again, let's draw the contrast here.

1. Writing, thinking, and dialoging with yourself are part of living whether you are creating or not. By giving some process to this inner stream of consciousness, by making the subconscious conscious, we can pull that energy and those ideas into our work.

2. Talking with another person about writing, painting, or composing, however fun and fulfilling it might seem at the time, is a dissipative process. When you get jazzed up from telling about the idea, you are letting out a lot of the energy necessary to complete the work on the idea.

If your goal is to create beautiful finished pieces of work, or continue on and create a body of work, you need to STFU and do the work. Celebrate at the gallery opening, record release party, book signing. But keep the celebration of the work inside you until that particular piece of work is done.

A fascinating thing happens when you contain the energy this way: the momentum and energy grows. You want to share your ideas. That's why you are striving to be an artist, to share, to create, to expand. But until your "piece" is done, keep that energy and momentum to yourself. Do morning pages as a process and see how your inner dialogue strengthens. And finally, get your butt in the seat and do the work.

That is the goal of these letters. To show you ways to get your creativity flowing. But if you don't put the brush, the guitar, the keyboard in your hand, you're just thinking or talking about it.

Don't talk, do.

Don't think, take action.

Don't look for appreciation, let your own inner joy be all the appreciation you need to get the work finished.

Then, when the piece is done, you can celebrate a milestone along your path down the artist's way.

8

Cutting Deep to Find Your Genius

The deeper you can cut, the closer you get to the heart.

It is important to cut deep when you are learning your craft. If you shy away from the harder, darker, deeper expressions, you may not find your way beyond the surface expression. Think of the love poem as an example. If we take the easy road, we may find lovely expressions of beauty, affection, joy, exhilaration. But perhaps this is more the love poetry of our childhood, rather than the poetic expression of rip-roaring love.

Let's look at two examples:

This is more of a love greeting card than a deep expression of emotion. It's fine to begin here, to start with this type of expression, but it takes no risks, it uses ordinary language. And this type of "poem" is fairly lifeless. Your sweetheart might enjoy the sweet card on Valentine's Day, but this type of poem was better in elementary school.

Now let's find a short example of a poet who takes a deeper cut at love.

You are a sky of autumn, pale and rose;
But all the sea of sadness in my blood
Surges, and ebbing, leaves my lips morose,
Salt with the memory of the bitter flood.

– the eyes of beauty, Baudelaire

This poem may not be to your taste, but you get the full

thrust of his longing and ache of his love and lust. You get oceans, and blood, and salt. He has truly opened a vein and let a bit of his heart spill out on the page. This is your task. Find the vein that you are able to access and give us the deepest cut you can at the turmoil love brings into all you think, and do, and feel. Safe expression of love is not very interesting. We all have this opportunity, and we can get it in the birthday card aisle at the grocery store. This is not the realm of art.

If you are looking for art and wanting to find a your unique voice, you have to bypass inhibition and go for the darkness, the real free-falling, the overwhelming sensations that you cannot control. Even in your art (visual, musical, textual) you must lose control. It's the controlled loss of control that creates great art.

Think of your top inspirations in creative expression. Most of them learned to cut directly through their own editors to unleash a torrent of emotion that could not be contained or edited. It's more like a flood when you hit the rich gold of deep expression.

Some of our best and deepest artists tapped into that expression beyond the conscious or rational control. It is in the risking, the dare you take to go further and farther into your obsession and give us a glimpse of the ecstasy or agony that is roiling inside. I think of Robert Motherwell's explosive ink paintings as a fine example of letting go, exploding, pouring out something darker and deeper than words could express.

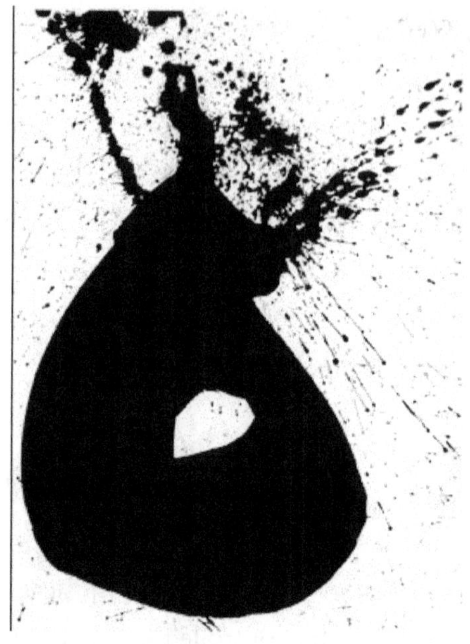

What he gives us is the controlled lack of control. Something random and dark that he released as finished and complete. He dared us to look into child-like expressions and see the art, the love, the power of the gesture. He is not saying, "Look at my genius, look at my love or my artistic expression." In most of his work, his genius was letting go, showing us how to release anything and everything with abandon.

Your job, as a young artist, is to learn to let go. Find your way to the depths of expression and pull up any small bits you can. The more pure and raw, the more original and striking the better. You can afford to fail at your age. Try and dig deep. Go fearlessly into the abyss and pull back some of the cold, black mud from the bottom, then toss it at your virtual canvas and step back.

One of the hardest lessons you must get in going deep is to turn off the editor while you create. You can edit later. But while you are plumbing the depths, you might hear yourself saying, "This is stupid. This is gross. This makes no sense." At this point thank your editor for the information and press on. Imagine the first moment Robert Motherwell blasted a white canvas with black ink and said, "DONE."

He was pioneering some radical notion that this minimal, child-like gesture could be ART. And as an adult man attempting to establish his genius and find his unique expression, he was taking a great risk. But the more he poured out on the canvas, the more he must have felt the rush of exposure. The more he ripped at the canvas, added color and shape without any prior guidelines, the more he knew he had tapped a deep vein of expression.

You've got to find your vein. And, pardon the expression, you've got to spill it out all over the page.

9

Vocation and Passion

We've got to talk about money for a minute.

I know, it sometimes seems like the antithesis of art, but it's something that must be addressed if you are going to survive. A long time ago, primarily in Europe, artists had benefactors and commissions. And some were set free by this accommodation. Many wrote, played, and created for their champions, and we've never heard from them again. There is a fine mix between money and art. And if you don't get the blend right, you might find yourself writing or creating things that no longer resemble art but look more like advertisements or vanity pronouncements.

One thing is certain, you have to figure out your money. Without it, life is hard. And in extreme cases it does more than crush your creative dreams, it can drive even the most creative and prolific artist into depression and even death. We don't want to go there. The tortured artist mode is better as an affectation and not a reality. Let's avoid the starving artist mode as much as possible. As long as that premise is okay with you, we can continue…

You can decide to make a living with your art, or you can decide, as I did, to make your art in spite of making a living.

When I was working at an advertising firm in my 20s I began taking Master of Fine Arts (MFA) classes at a nearby college. I didn't want to teach, I wanted to write. And the environment of college is a great time and place to be productive and supported as an artist. The only problem is, college costs money. And the terminal path of the MFA is teaching. And teaching doesn't pay much, and the job market for writing, painting, creativity teachers is awful. Hear me. You will likely starve to death by going down the teaching path. Too few jobs, too many MFAs (you might as well get a PhD while you're at it, to delay your real task of making a living), and a starting pay scale that might keep you in ramen but won't afford you the aperitif and Starbucks life you might aspire to.

And I'm not saying you can't do it. What I'm saying is the odds are against making a comfortable living as a teacher of the creative arts. The competition is as fierce for the jobs as it is for publication in the *New Yorker*. It happens. And new writers do get published in the *New Yorker*, but they are competing with the hottest and most established writers in the country for the few weekly openings. And at some level, that tier of publishing is about networks and connections more than the writing.

So what I want to say, and what rang true for me when I started taking MFA classes, is that you *can* go the teaching-to-creative-artist route, but it's a long shot. And more often you will end your college degree with a nice loan payment and no job to start paying it with. So you might be working at Starbucks (they have great insurance) rather than enjoying a latte on the Champs-Élysées. So let's look at the other options.

The head of the MFA program at this small school agreed to meet me for beers one evening after our class. We had a nice chat. He is one of the winners. He was a tenured professor at the head of an MFA program. Not one you've ever heard of, but he was working AND writing, so let's say he was a home run hitter. And across the table over craft beers, he said something profound. "Keep your job," he said, referring to my gig at the advertising agency. "You're making more money there than you ever will as a teacher, and that's IF you could find the job. And that's the lie. There just aren't very many teaching jobs for writers. And even the top 5% of graduates from the Iowa Writer's Workshop will be competing for small college assistant professorships with no tenure."

Crap.

"So if you want to write," he continued. "Then write. But don't quit your day job."

Hell.

I had been talking about my job and how I was jealous of the students who were full time at the university. I was contemplating taking a two-year sabbatical and going to school full time again. He advised against it. "There just aren't any jobs. It's a lie. We're selling a dream that doesn't exist. Most of these kids will be working at jobs that have nothing to do with writing. And you are already there."

Cheers.

I thanked him and walked away fairly defeated. (Maybe that's how you're feeling now, as you were contemplating your "creative" degree program.) But I have never forgotten his advice.

Okay, so let's look at the other path. The non-creative job path. This is how I have survived. I did keep the advertising job. And while I completed the "creative" sequence of the MFA program, I dropped my first academic class the next semester. I didn't want to write another research paper, EVER. So I didn't. I walked away. And there really was no further I could go at this university without changing plans. The professor is still there. And he's published three books in the15 years since our discussion. I really should look him up. He was also my favorite teacher.

In all the doubts you have ahead of you about your craft, let's take money out of the equation. If you are looking to make a living on your art (writing, music, painting), you have a long road ahead. The path is lined with many success stories. And I won't discourage you from giving it the old college try. (Well, except for the post-graduate college thing, don't do that, unless you have to.) But what I'm going to suggest to you is find your vocation along with your passion. If you can do something well, that relates to a specific business objective, you can find a working-for-a-living role somewhere. For me it was advertising. More specifically, digital marketing.

I shied away from copywriting because I didn't really want to crowd out my flowery language with headlines and slogans. I didn't even really want to do jingles and start mixing in my musical ambitions with the crap you hear on the radio. Nope. I made my initial run at advertising through the design and production artist route. So I was a designer and desktop publisher. And as I have grown and aged, I have continued to hone my digital skills along with my writing and composing skills.

And here's the thing you need to be clear about. If your goals are having a family, a house, proper clothing, insurance, food, and shelter, then you need to look at your career as something slightly different from your passion. And it's not that I'm not passionate about digital marketing. I am quite passionate about it. But I'm more passionate about writing. Stories, novels, poems, journals. And creating music in all its glorious forms.

You are young, you are just starting college consideration. And your musical talents are starting to rise. You've got it. I'm telling you you have something quite special in all that you do. BUT… you've still got to make a living. Just put that in your hopper for a minute as you contemplate the next five to eight years of your life.

And the words of that professor may help here. "Do your work. You're making good money. You're making a living. If you still have the energy to write and be creative, then put the rest of your focus there. If you are a writer, you're going to write. Nothing will stop you. But why starve to death while doing it?"

He was a living example of success. And he was wearing a threadbare tweed jacket (standard college professor issue) and happy to have me pay for the two beers. I love him and all that he stood for. He was the head of an MFA program. He had made it. His writing was fantastic. And at 28 years old, I was already making more money than he was. He steered me back towards my career and what I could do for a living. "Then write your ass off. You're always going to have the writing."

And that's sort of where I am today. I've been doing digital marketing for the past 15 years. And I've had various spurts and leaps in creativity. I wrote my first full novel (unpublished), a play, a screenplay, a musical, and a lot of short stories. And the real joy: I have two kids, a nice car, and a comfortable living. I have questioned my path all the time. And as an artist this is a frequent struggle. You will often question your commitment to art. And you may give it up. You may walk away and go into accounting or law. That's okay. But the writer, the artist, and the musician are always going to find ways to do their art.

If you are an artist, your path is to survive. If you can survive and be happy as a musician playing nightly gigs and living with roommates for a while, then go for it. But if you want a home and kids and nicer things that aren't off Craigslist, then you might consider your vocation as a path to support your passion.

Again, I want to be clear. Art is hard. And you will have challenges all your life as an artist. But the biggest challenge may be how to survive, how to make a living, and how not to compromise your long-term vision. The two things have to coexist: work and art. And figuring out the mix that works for you is one of the grand mysteries of life. When you have found your way, you will have both enough money to be happy with what you have and the energy to continue creating your art until the world finally steps up and recognizes you with fame and ultimately money.

If you've got a benefactor, great. If you can squeeze out a graduate degree from your parents without putting yourself in major debt, perhaps that's the way to nurture and hone your craft. But ultimately you have to find a way to make a living. That's the prime task of the artist. Your art will continue to come. Your poems, songs, stories, paintings will never be exhausted. You have your entire life to create. But if you run completely out of money, both your craft and your life are going to suffer greatly.

I don't believe in the "starving artist" ethic. I think you can both make a living and make art. It's a magic trick to figure it out. But that's my goal. I'm still working on it.

Carry on. Follow your heart. You are young, and you have years to figure this out. But keep your career in mind when choosing your paths over the next few years. College is an awesome time, and you CAN lock in some of your craft while heading towards your vocation. But don't drop out too far into the artist mode and forget the worker mode. You have got to have both.

I believe in you.

10

Sing at the Top of Your Range

Now is the time for you to sing at the top of your range. Go deep. Go long. Go silly and serious and dark and beautiful. Go crazy. Now is the time in your life when you can afford to lose everything over and over again in your art. Don't shy away from the deepest cut. Leap towards the abyss, the highs, the lows, the mountains you want to climb, and the deep ocean rifts you need to explore.

As you are developing into a young artist, you have the opportunity to learn how to soar. Go for it. There is brilliance in reckless abandon. Later in your life, risks will be less inviting. As you settle into your adult life, plenty of pressures will be driving you away from your passionate heart and back into the little box of making a living, of paying bills, of doing what you are supposed to do. While you can afford to be indulgent, do it with heart and fearlessness.

What do you have to fear? What's the loss of trying for the ultimate love song and missing by a few Lennons? There is no shame in a failed love song. And as you fail over and over again, you may even get closer to tasting the beauty and passion you are trying to unlock. You may have the opportunity, at this early period in your life, to experience love at a sublime, sublingual level. You may be able to touch the heart of someone else with your honesty and openness. Don't despair if they ran away when you shared your love song. Or don't share them yet. It is your choice. You will have many opportunities to love deeply and fail, both at the relationship and the songs that result from the disaster.

I'm not being cynical here. You are on this planet to express your loves and losses. You are a gift. Your expression of true feelings helps others explore the depths of their own hearts and aches. The closer you get to capturing the raw power of this love, both in ascension and the arc back towards Earth, the closer you are to creating a work of art. Give yourself fully to the feelings and fully to the expression of those feelings from the artist's eye. Whatever your art, give the canvas a full range of emotion. Blood red strokes of love and passion and cutting to the quick may be your genius. It is too early for you to know.

It is too early for anyone to know if they are becoming a great artist. It is only necessary to try. To aspire to great expressions. And I can see that you have that gift. Even in learning and singing a favorite song by someone else, you have an ability to make it your own. You can give us the gift of the song and the singer anytime, and in the moment, at this time of your life and development, it doesn't matter too greatly if the song you sing is someone else's or your own. A singer always looks for the greatest song, the largest expression of emotion and range and depth.

Find your voice. In song, word, or visual art, find YOUR voice. Part of that discovery is learning how to let go of the editor, the objections, the resistance to going long and deep. Unleashing the artist has a lot to do with silencing the negative self-talk that recommends less honesty, less revelation, and more common, or safe, expression. But no great love song was born out of playing it safe. Love is not safe. Art is not safe either. It is necessary to get a little blood on the tracks in order to know what pain and suffering feel like. It is okay. You will heal. But your broken love song may be the key that unlocks the flip side, the happy expression of love. This is much rarer and harder to achieve. You must try both.

The Beatles' song, "I Saw Her Standing There," is one of my favorite high-on-love-and-youth-and-beauty love songs. There is magic in the simple expression of joy/awe/self-awareness and then letting the listener in on the magic. In the song we get the line, "Well she was just 17/ if you know what I mean," and we *all* know what he means. Such a simple moment. And the first two lines of the song. And like that, the entire landscape of the love song and our participation as observers in the act of the singer falling in love with a girl in a club.

Go find your 17. Go be silly. Write, create, dream, and do it with every ounce of your fiber. Then, if you can, let a tiny sliver of it out as an expression of your craft. Be pure and clear. The more honest you can be, the more it will resonate with the rest of us. You may not have had your "17" moment, but you will. And when you do, whenever you do, milk it for the seeds of emotion that are the universal truths of love, youth, beauty, a first kiss, and falling hard for someone you've just met. If you can write one "I Saw Her Standing There" in your lifetime, you will have accomplished a rare honor.

But don't give up when it gets hard. It will get hard. The girl will leave. The song will not come out right. The fame and fortune won't come in the way you'd hoped. This is all part of the process of tempering your sword/pen/brush. This is all part of either becoming an artist or giving up the dream of becoming one. It is okay if you turn to finance or business as your life's work. And perhaps those old songs you wrote in your youth will still give you a grin. Maybe your kids will get a kick out of the videos of your young bands and how funny you looked.

And it's okay to leave the art behind. If that's your path, you will still be well served to have given voice to that deep expression of love, and youth, and artful struggle.

If you continue to create, however, these early attempts will provide the bedrock and the seeds of what you may be capable of in your lifetime. Art is about persistence. Longevity is the only key you can control. If you never give up, you will continue to BE an artist your entire life. And for me, that is the goal.

Sure, I longed for fame, fortune, and groupies when I was playing in my college bands. And even as I started a new family, with a son and a baby on the way, I was hopeful that my band would make the big time. Of course, you know, we didn't. Or I might be playing Red Rocks tonight rather than writing you this letter.

But I am still striving to write a perfect love song. And the songs and attempts at profound beauty of my earlier years are still rattling around in my mind as I go for the next lyric. Every attempt is a good attempt. Even writing a string of crappy love songs gives us, as artists, a gift. We learn what is easy. We learn what is more difficult. And we attempt what is forbidden or dark or previously unexpressed. Genre doesn't matter if you are creating a valid and lasting expression of genius.

And that's really what your goal is at this early stage of your life: try everything and listen for where your genius comes to life. You will know it when the energy hits. You will not be able to deny your gift when you begin to feel the powerful thoughts, hopes, and dreams that begin to flood your waking and sleeping moments. When you tap into your gift, you will be unable to stop it. This is the gift and the goal of an artist's life. Find the gold in your expression, the gold you yourself appreciate, and you will never stop mining for more.

I wish you happiness, pain, and healing, and all the expressions of your art that are in between, beyond, and just ahead of you. And I wish for you to find your genius and know it. From this self-awareness you can continue to attempt the mountaintop for the rest of your life.

May you never stop seeking the top.

11

Creative Energy: Finding and Maintaining Your Daily Juice

Getting through the day, every day, is a trick.

Either you are energetic or you aren't. Your daily cadence and the management of your energy throughout your day are among the most important pillars of your creative life. If you are tired, you may still be able to be creative, but your output and optimism will suffer. You have got to find what works for you. And perhaps what's working for you now, youth and hopefulness, may fade over the years, and you will have to find other circuits for your "juice."

Here are a few of the things that can provide energy:

- Coffee

- Getting enough rest

- Inspiration
- A good conversation with a friend
- A burning desire
- Love
- Angst
- Raw fruit juices
- Fasting
- Running
- Meditating
- Sex
- Swimming
- Paleo diet
- Sugar
- A relationship
- Loneliness
- New love
- A melody
- Collaboration
- Experiencing another artist's joy
- A found word, object, melody, image
- Correspondence with another artist
- Imagining your own success

- Vitamins
- Drugs
- Not enough sleep
- Dancing
- Going for a walk
- Playing a sport
- Winning at a sport or game
- An imaginary structure for your creative work (a series, a triptych, a musical)
- Praise
- A like-minded friend
- Activism
- A burning desire to tell your story
- The perfect slice of watermelon on a hot summer's day

All of these things, or the lack of these things, can influence your daily energy. And the trajectory of your daily rush, the blood sugar coursing through your veins, gives the power (or lack of power) to drive your creative vision forward. A lot of your task in life is to figure out how to light your own locomotive engine inside and then keep it stoked and roaring down the tracks. And also learning what puts out, or disspates the fire, momentum, rush towards the light at the other end of the tunnel.

If you are only rushing down the tracks to achieve fame, you've got a long tunnel ahead, indeed. But if you are making art that you believe in, the act of creating itself becomes the track, and the tunnel, and the light at the other end. If you are creating out of an inner fire and inner need to create, you can regulate your burn rate and consumption more carefully. You can set your sights on the next destination in your mind and celebrate your own victory at each passing station.

Life is a very long trip. Finding what supports your energy is one of the most important tasks you can master. You then can choose to use different "juices" to different effects. Sometimes burning the candle on both ends is what will serve your idea. Sometimes getting to bed by 10:00 p.m. and arising to create by 5:30 in the morning is what will get your vision further down the track.

Build your Grand Central Station of art for yourself. When other visitors come through, let them be amazed at your ingenuity and flair. But don't slow down too much to listen to the praise or criticism. Grab a handful of the fuel of your day and get back on the tracks towards your next creation. Through this forward momentum, and daily management of your fuel, you can sustain your creative work throughout your lifetime.

Find your juice. Support your energy. Do the work.

12

Get Into Your Mess: Cleaning Can Be a Distraction

In my life and my art, some of my best moments are very messy. If I stopped after every session to clean it all back up, well, I'd be spending a lot of time cleaning. Yes, occasionally my studio or office gets a little chaotic for my tastes. When my productivity gets slowed down by piles of ideas, or clothes on top of my recording equipment (not for sound dampening), then I know it's time to put things in piles elsewhere.

I know when I was a kid I was like this. When I would get a "project" going, I'd have ideas and parts all over my room. And sure enough, my mom would come by at some point and say, "You need to pick all that up, you know." Buzz kill.

Even as a young person, I knew she was controlling me and my messy madness.

Okay, so Mom's not here anymore. We're still compelled, occasionally, to clean and organize and fold every thing right out of the dryer. But it's not really all that conducive to creativity for me. Sometimes I like to start with an empty and clean desk. But I also like to leave projects open and half-completed, almost as if they are calling me back. "Come look at this idea, plug the guitar back in, let's have another run at this one."

So, compulsive cleaning and hyper-organization can be a distraction. You can avoid sitting in the chair and writing, if you feel you absolutely must make up your bed and pick up the books off the floor. But… do you need to? Or are you avoiding the more difficult prospect of facing your creativity head on?

We all have lots of reasons for not doing our art. Fear. Money. Time. Relationships. No relationship. Depression. And cleaning your room can be one of those that's more of a hold over from your little person times, when your mom had more sway than she does now.

Here's a shot of Kurt Vonnegut working in his home.

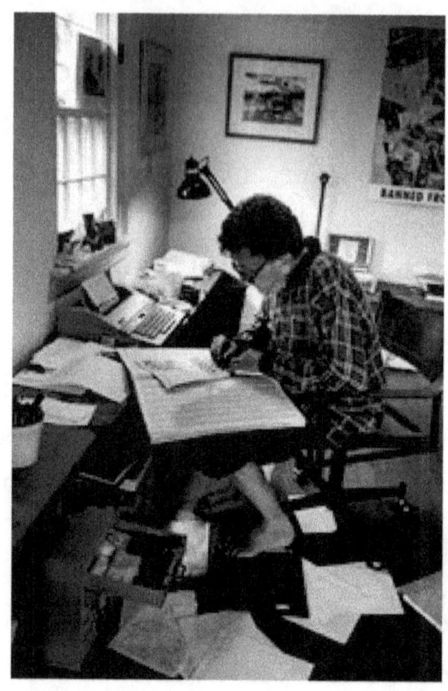

"You think it's messy out here?" he said, smiling.
Then he pointed to his head. "You should see what it
looks like in here."

Get over your childhood ideas about your messy room or your messy habits. A messy studio is an active studio. A pristine desk or pristine painter's studio is not in use. You want to put your creatitivy to use. If you're always cleaning up, how do you pick up again on a project that wasn't fully baked yet? You don't.

Let your mess show. Let your creativity bloom in any direction it needs to go. Don't worry about Mom. Read her this letter when she complains to you. You deserve to get your creativity all over you and all over your room. Do it. Clean up if you have to, or clean up as a celebration for the completion of some massive project you've been working and messing on. Let your mess be a pressure to keep you focused on completing. You can't clean until you complete.

Don't let your compulsive cleanliness get in the way of your soaring inspirations. "Just close the door, Mom," is a fine answer. (Even if Mom is just an idea in your head.)

Note: Image: Vonnegut at work, Write Place, Write Time blog, Creative Commons usage

13

Solitude and the Artistic Temperament

Pass through the darkness. Embrace the dark nights of your soul as they have arrived to tell you something.

We've got to talk about the dark side for a moment. If you've got a handful of guiding artists that you look to for inspiration, you're likely to have a few that succumbed to the flipside of massive inspiration: massive depression. The literary and artistic cannon is filled with tragic artists.

Let's recognize the pattern and align ourselves with the survivors.

Understanding the highs and lows of my creative life has been an interesting journey. I have traveled both high and low roads. I've sat on mountaintops and done vision quests.

I've spent countless hours in talk therapy and counseling of many types. I've read deeply of the artists who spoke to the blackness of my own journey and tried to learn from their ultimate loss. My list is long, but the top-of-mind artists who continue to inspire me, in spite of their demise (via alcohol, suicide, or mental illness), are Jack Kerouac, Sylvia Plath, Elliot Smith, David Foster Wallace, Hemingway, and Anne Sexton. And in my own personal life, my older sister, who was creating at the top of her game, took her life when some of the details of reality became too hard to bear.

But bear it we must. That's the ticket, that's the key.

- Perseverance in the face of great odds. (You will probably not achieve the recognition or fame you desire with your art.)

- Mental stability in the heat of creative passion. (I still have to dial my own flights of fantasy back when I'm in the throes of a passionate project.)

- Emotional fortitude even while dipping into the darkness that often illuminates or transforms our work. (Embrace the darkness, don't be embraced by it.)

- Financial plans and career maps. (If you're not making money, you're going to starve. That's a path heading in the wrong direction.)

- Joyful rebalancing. (The joy in your life is your energy. Find ways to rebalance, or self-regulate, your attitude, constantly.)

We can learn a lot from the deep passion of these creative souls. Even if a few of them dipped too far into the dark night of the soul, you will eventually have to deal with your own inner demons. We've all got them.

Life throws us all types of curveballs. And life is messy. You know some of the tragedies that are ahead: the death of a parent, a beloved pet, the loss of a primary relationship. Many dark curves you cannot see but will throw you off your joyous course for a time. It is my artistic temperament that allows me to absorb and be burnished by these events, and in the polishing and blasting of the sadness and fear, I believe, I am transformed.

The death of my father when I was 21 is an event that I will never fully get over. But the transformation of that event into stories, songs, and perhaps even a novel at some point is one of the ways I have found my own strength in not following his will ("Why aren't you going to medical school?") or his demise as he used more alcohol to distract him from the wreckage of his alcoholic life. I tumbled in the rock-polishing machine for most of my 20s, I railed and ranted in my 30s, and here in my 50s I'm happy to report that I'm drug and disease free and of relatively sound mind and body.

I say "relatively" only to be dramatic. No one is actually 100% healthy. We've all got hurt places, little secrets, jealousies, resentments, and vendettas we'd like to see paid in full. And each of us had a choice to walk the higher road above our own petty grievances or to fall victim to the angry path through our perceived injustices. The injustices are all around us. Our personal stories are not that unique until we tell them through our art. And in that exposure we might find relief, or at least camaraderie.

The work of these previous sojourners can provide some comfort. Some of them may be too close for comfort. Either way, you will go through dark times. Your artistic translation of these horrific events into art provides (a) comfort for you, (b) comfort for others, and (c) something of lasting beauty and value. Dwelling in the darkness for a time may serve you well. We certainly can agree that running from your emotional messiness is not an option; the anger, fear, and sadness WILL catch up with you.

It's okay to be dark. It's okay to require professional help. It's okay to struggle for a time with your own personal demons. The world outside our souls is often troublesome, even in the best of times. In my past, when things got really hard, however, it was my art that kept me pointed upward and onward, even when I lacked any inspiration or motivation to do much more than noodle on a poem or pluck a few strings on my guitar.

Pass through the darkness. Embrace the dark nights of your soul as they have arrived to tell you something, to transform your life into something more beautiful. Please don't lose yourself in the darkness. Too many wonderful and talented artists have chosen the most unromantic ways to take their last curtain calls. Suicide is never romantic nor epic. The loss of so many beautiful artists illuminates our lack of understanding and support for the highs and lows of our creative people. Be creative. Be dark. But stay alive and tell us about your journey.

Even as we lose lovers, parents, siblings, we have the ability to translate our suffering into expressions of love and beauty. Listen to your dark whisperings; ignoring them will shut down an entire cathedral of creativity and inspiration that can speak to all of us at some point in our lives. Life is that way: messy, painful, unexplainable. Artists merely try to deal with these uncertainties and losses by telling their own version of Dante's *Inferno*.

14

Artistic Depression: There's Nothing Romantic About it

What if artistic depression was a response to the existential experience of being an artist and not being paid for what you do? What if depression was unnecessary for the creation of art?

We like to think of our depressed artists as going through some romantic struggle to produce their art. Turns out, depression is not part of the creative process. Plenty of creative geniuses have never suffered from clinical depression. And plenty of our clinically depressed geniuses might have lived a lot longer had they not been struggling with the black beast of the dog.

I'm going to try to illuminate a few things about art and depression that may help further this discussion.

In his seminal book *Against Depression,* Dr. Kramer does a great job of bringing to light two different ideas.

1. While he was traveling around presenting his first book, *Talking to Prozac,* Dr. Kramer started trying on this question: "If you could eliminate depression with a single pill, a new magic treatment, would you use it?" He was surprised by the number of doctors who said they would not use the magic cure for depression, fearing the loss of the creative or romantic output of the struggling artist. Would we have Starry Night if not for depression? The premise is false. Depression did not create those masterpieces. It was depression that cut them off, that cut down these artists before their prime. Eliminating depression would not have prevented Starry Night from happening, it might have allowed for version 2 and version 3. But we'll never get to see those creations.

2. Depression, like an illness, actually makes physical changes in the human brain. This fact was important, as the discussion about behavior versus illness still runs rampant. The argument goes, if like an illness, we can see the changes in the physical body of the suffering patient, we can claim depression as a traditional illness and provide better treatment and insurance coverage. But the point is this: as a person experiences massive depressions as a result of some traumatic event, the physical pathways in their brains begin to lean towards

depression. It's as if the "depression neural pathways" get strengthened in the course of several depressions.

In my case, this strengthening was a propensity towards giving up. Simply feeling like I could not go on, I could not be successful at my chosen endeavor, and therefore I should just give up. As I suffered, in my early teens, some major traumas, my brain learned to light up the helpless pathway. The give-up pathway. I'm still unlearning this response. I am actively trying to strengthen the alternative responses. The good news is the brain can change. Plasticity means the brain can unlearn these depression tendencies.

Just like I go for a tangerine rather than a piece of pie, my brain can be trained to look at setbacks and stresses as a trigger for action rather than a slip into hopelessness and inaction. I have to be aware of what's happening, I have to be very conscious and vigilant, but I can short-circuit the tendency towards folding. Instead, I'm learning to use my creativity (journaling) to write about the depressed feelings as they are occurring. Thus, I'm attempting to illuminate the old thinking and focus on the new options.

Part of being an artist is dealing with the fact that we also have to find a way (outside our art) to make a living. We could choose to be starving artists, I suppose, but no one really sets out to be poor. More likely, if you commit the time required to become a great musician, for example, the opportunities to become famous, and thus rewarded for your musical talents and practice, you still will need a day job. And the future of creative economics is getting worse, not better.

But this is not a reason to fall into habits of despair and hopelessness. Nope. To be an artist, you first have to desire your art over everything else, occasionally even companionship and exercise.

The artistic challenge in life is not just to master your art and your self-discipline, it's to find a way to earn a living that does not crush the life out of you and your creative passion. A lot of this is in your mind. I go to a job every day. The job is one of the paths towards securing the time in my life that I need to create my music or my writing. I can complain about the job, and The Man getting me down, or the sorry state of selling recorded music online, or I could just stay focused on the act of creation.

If you believe in what you are creating, nothing can stand between you and your work. The money will come. And until it does, the job is what you must have. The job allows you to live a lifestyle of leisure, the time off you actually do require to do your work. The first thing that goes when I'm under stress about money, or depressed, is my ability to create works of art.

I have to solve the survival needs first. Once I have begun to master food, clothing, and shelter, I can begin to write songs and poems to put in my house.

Depression is not a key or romantic partner of creativity. And money is not the root of all evil (*love* of money is). But we have to come to terms with both our highs and lows. We have to find a way to make a living while we create our masterpiece.

Don't give up just because you are not making money. Don't give up because you might not be discovered in your lifetime. Don't give up because you must create. If you have the burning desire to write, paint, sing, play, keep going. Put the poems in a folder. Put the songs in a collection and release them. Have an art opening, regardless of how many people come or if you sell a single piece.

We've got romantic ideas about sadness or depression and its connection to the creative/artistic spirit. It's a bullshit notion. And we've got the exact opposite impression when it comes to money. Working for a corporation is "always" working for The Man. But what if working for the company gives you the house to live in, the insurance for the kids you want, and the ability to NOT work on the weekends, when you drink your cup of coffee and stay up late creating, even when no one is listening, watching, or buying your art?

15

Survive and Thrive: First Find Your Congregation Within

When the money runs out, my inspiration gets pretty desperate. Entire creative cannons in motion and lit up begin to crumble as I doubt myself. And trying to push into the creative as an income stream, for me, has never worked. I'm not interested in being a starving artist. So one of the first struggles, for me, is making sure I have my bills covered.

There are a million paths to creative success, but money may not be one of them for many of us. Once you get that concept fully swallowed, you can get on with the work of making your art, whatever that is. Sure, you'll have to find the "day job," but you can do that. That's one of the base levels of survival as an artist.

Of course there are paths to use your creative craft as a job, but I've seen too many copywriters, too many cover band musicians who are doing just that: the job has become the creative outlet. Let me take an example from my home town. Charlie Sexton is an amazing performer, singer, songwriter, guitar player. And how can you blame him for going out on the road with Bob Dylan? See the world, be semi-famous under the hot spotlights alongside the legend himself. Sure, no problem. But where's the next Charlie Sexton album?

And a second example came when I was chatting with one of my favorite cover band leaders. I asked him, "So when's your next record coming out?"

He looked at me with a smile, but he seemed to be hiding something a bit deeper. "When I feel a bit less content, I guess."

That is also a hard one. Contentment versus Creative Drive. Can the two forces exist together? Can you be supremely content and still have the drive to create new works of art? Or is the creative production tied up in the discontentment, the angst and struggle of life? I've had problems with this in the past. I needed some goal to get me out of my current situation as a catalyst. Like the situation I was in was not enough, so I needed to produce my art to affirm my ever-burning quest to be someone else, someone huge and successful.

But I was/am successful in my mind. I have two great kids. I'm growing creatively and as a parent. And while I'm somewhat content, I'm also driven to express my art. At this point in my life, I'm not looking for any money from the effort. I've disconnected my art from my income needs. This was a major win for me.

I say somewhat content, because there are plenty of things in my life that are way out of balance. I'm working on those. And this week I signed a contract, not for a record deal, but for a work deal that's going to fill up my work card for the next few months in a big way. And this WIN is actually giving me some energetic leeway to drive forward with my musical projects at the same time. See, having some financial success in my "career" is actually generating some creative energy in my other career.

And then there are the writers, artists, and creatives who have lost faith in their craft. This is the more common story. Somewhere along life, the act of growing up has dampened our dreams of rock stardom. And unfortunately, stardom is so rare that most of my friends who are creative have left their instruments and paintbrushes behind. The focus on work, life, money, kids, housing… It's not easy. But the formula is easy.

Survival + Passion + Longevity = A Creative Life

I'm not looking to be a rock star. I might have had those delusions back in my teens. But I was more interested in capturing the perfect song or short story. I learned to work to support my art and not the other way around.

If you can get your survival needs met and keep your passion for the voice that is inside of you trying to express some kind of beauty, you will either persevere or you won't. And that's okay. It is fine when people leave music, poetry, painting, writing, behind. It's not for everyone. And if it was a hobby, then perhaps there are other things in life that give you more satisfaction. Parenting can have a profound effect on your life and your creative output.

My kids, however, only inspired me more. I wanted to include them in my musical life. I wanted to surround them with songs, mine and others. I wanted to show them my songs, I wanted to serenade them all the time. (I even imagined a kid's record, but there were so many that I loved already…) And in learning to work, parent, and continue to give time to my music, I started creating a lifestyle formula that worked for me. Today my son is an accomplished violinist, and my daughter sings in the choir. (She won't join me on stage, however, because she claims to have performance anxiety. Oh well, maybe later.)

The part I got right is the survival. I do have a career. And when I structure things right, I can work with a bit of flexibility that allows me occasional inspirational afternoons and nights, even in the middle of the week. When I get out of balance, I begin aspiring towards rock stardom again and I stop making my "work" the priority. That has been an issue for me in the past, but I'm pretty good at managing it these days.

The humorous rejoinder, "Don't quit your day job," has never been more appropriate. But the corollary, however, is more important: "Don't stop believing in your art."

Figure out how to make a living. Find a place for your art in the daily cadence of your life. And never give it up. You'll be fine then, regardless of any outside, perceived success or fame.

16

The Creative Impulse: Easy to Contain, Easier to Kill

It is much easier to ignore our creative impulses than to indulge in the craft of trying to bring them to life. That's a real problem for a writer, painter, or musician. The little spark of an idea must be captured and fanned until it catches fire and becomes a story, painting, or song. It is the turning away from our creative impulses that can become an issue.

There are a lot of demands on our time. There is the demand to make money if we want to eat and have a place to live. There is the demand to be a parent and a partner if we have families. There is a demand for sleep, and food, and exercise. And if you can attend to all that and carve out some time that you are not exhausted, well… usually it is in this "after time" that we can indulge our craft.

When I was married with children I used to work on my music and writing between 10:00 p.m. and 2:00 a.m. It was the only window of time, after we had put the kids down for bed, that allowed me the long stretch of quiet time to engage with my creative muse. It wasn't easy. My then-wife would complain if I didn't help enough around the house. My job demanded I be sharp and not burned out. And some nights I would play video games rather than "create" because I was just too exhausted.

But the commitment to the craft was important to me. And the commitment today is even stronger. That is because I am nurturing the creative voice in my life. I am listening for the creative impulses and trying to go with the flow. I'm not always successful, but I'm always trying.

The other morning, before work, I was struck by a song idea that wouldn't be tamed. And I thought I had my music capture method down. I recorded some guitar parts into Garageband. Or did I put them on video on my phone? Hmmm. Anyway, during the course of the morning I was uber-inspired, so I also wrote down the lyrics about an hour later. Everything was flowing. But… I was running out of time. I had a meeting I had to attend in person.

Here is where the problem is.

I tried to capture all the parts of the song, but just as I should've recorded a single, guitar-voice version, I didn't. I imagined that my multiple capture points had gotten enough of the creative impulse for me to recreate the feeling several days later when I came back to the idea. I was wrong.

The "several days later" became more than a week. And when I finally carved out a few hours on a Sunday afternoon, there was no amount of coffee or enthusiasm that could breathe life into my "parts." I was sad but not broken. Even in the recovery of ideas, it can still be a "moment" thing. I need to come back to that song idea when I'm fresh.

So even under the best circumstances, when you've harnessed the creative impulse and are well on your way to your next masterpiece, it is easy to get derailed. Even when you think you have all the pieces and parts and processes down. It really is "the moment" sometimes that requires the full attention. Delay and deflection of that creative drive will usually result in a less vibrant expression.

Keep your impulses high. When you have the gift of an idea, run with it until you capture as much of it as time will allow. And, in my experience, come back to the idea as soon as possible to reignite the threads of energy that began to weave into the creative work.

Write. Sing. Paint. Draw.

And do it as often as time will allow.

17

The Portable Artist: Creativity On-the-Go!

Can you take your creative work on the road? Occasionally I love to work in coffee shops. If I'm listening for the cadence of dialogue, I can merely take off my headphones and listen to the conversations around me. Need ideas? Listen.

With my first laptop computer (way back when), I had the ability to capture my thoughts, ideas, and narratives in a very powerful way. The laptop also gave me mobile access to music composition software. Although I've never gotten very good at that, the capture of musical ideas today has become more of a decision about which tool to use rather than how to capture it.

Apple's Music Notes is a great example of an app that gets out of the way to facilitate your creative expression. Open the app and you are presented with a single button: start recording. You then capture a musical idea via voice, guitar, piano, whatever. When you go to play it back, the app gives you some accompaniment options. Drums and guitar. Sometimes the results are useful, sometimes they are more humorous. But the point is, Apple's app allows you to record your idea. THEN it adds the fun.

You need to take your show on the road. If you're feeling stuck, get out of the state you're in, or at least get out of the house. Today's technology gives us so many ways to connect with our on creativity. And many more ways to connect with others.

Do you paint? Well, I suppose digital paint isn't quite the same thing. You might need a small watercolor set and a small pad. You need to keep refining your capture system.

As an example, this weekend, I had a song idea arrive at a very inconvenient moment. My girlfriend had just arrived home from a long run. She was interested in greetings. The song idea was just emerging. She saw the look on my face and gently closed the door on the office so I could continue. I used the video recorder on my phone and got the idea down right in that moment. And as I was capturing it, I was able to build up three distinct parts (verse, chorus, bridge). And even without knowing which was the chorus and which was the bridge, I was able to know that I had gotten the idea down.

I could then go greet my woman and go on with the rest of my day.

It is important that you can be flexible and agile with your capture system. If you're a painter, you may need to draw. A composer may need a simple recording program and some innovative input devices. The point is to make sure you can grab your system and go at a moment's notice. Then when the moment strikes, you can capture it and get back to the moments of your life.

18

What Will You Make Your Life About?

Always be arcing back towards what you want to be known for, for your heart's desire, for what gives you the most joy.

Finding your purpose sounds like a really daunting task, and I have run away from that phrase my entire life. But figuring out what my life is going to be about is easier to do.

Let's do some simple math around some of the big things my life COULD be about.

1. Marriage and kids (or divorce and kids, as in my case)
2. Career in ___ (today it's marketing, tomorrow it's writing)

3. Passion doing (today it's playing tennis and playing music)
4. Great at doing (marketing, writing, relationship navigation)

Today I would not say that my life is about writing, but it's going that way. Even this letter is another step in that direction. I am leaving behind a trail of words, songs, phrases that I hope, in the long run, define my full and happy life. My life today IS full and happy, but I'm still "working" at a number of things I'm good at, and a little bit passionate about, but they are not my life's work. Oh, those heavy phrases again. I'm not so much into "life's work" as finding my passion and letting that define my purpose.

I believe that my creative life is a celebration of the spiritual life I lead. I believe in God. And in that belief comes my understanding that my celebration of the human spirit (song, poem, drawing, anagram) is a celebration of God, or my God-given talents. And, of course, it's a lot more than talent, we've all got talent. My life well-lived is about commitment and tenacity. I will continue writing no matter what. And in my early 50s I'm quite confident that I'm writing better than I ever have. Stories I wanted to tell in my 20s and 30s are now within my narrative powers. Reading over my first novel, I'm excited to retell the entire tale from a more mature, more comprehensive perspective.

If you are the narrator of your life, what's the first line of your movie?

Here's a run at mine: "In 105 years, John McElhenney never quit writing songs and poems. He finished a new song hours before he fell asleep for the last time. Here's the last recording of Mr. McElhenney, a joyous love song to his wife."

Not bad.

What's your narrator going to say about your life in 20 years? Can you begin working towards a few of those ideals now? Can you arc your career closer to your passion? In my case, I am a writer. And while I've shied away from being a copy-writer, I have made a fairly good living writing words and building strategies for companies. I'd rather put my words to use for more enlightening subjects, but hey… we all gotta eat.

So how does my life stack up so far in my four categories?

1. Marriage and kids (35% of my time)
2. Career in ___ (50% of my time working)
3. Passion doing (5% of my time playing or writing)
4. Great at doing (10% of my time writing and building my empire)

It is my hope that I can continue to angle my life and work towards the fourth quadrant in my system. As I am gearing up for book proposals and screenplay submissions, it is a big hairy goal to write as my job. One breakaway title and I could do it. But I must keep my momentum up even without the fame and fortune. What I have in my court is that tenacity. I'm never going to stop writing. And as long as I keep getting better, in 10 years my writing is going to be amazing.

Do what you have to do to make a living and support the lifestyle you want to live. But always be arcing back towards what you want to be known for, for your heart's desire, for what gives you the most joy. That's the goal in life worth pursuing.

Coda: Love Money Ambition: Finding Your Sweet Spot and Career

"But what are you going to do for money?"

The question asked every second over the next few weeks as our kids head towards the summer and get done with their formal education. When I was in college, my dad would ask me this repeatedly. My English degree seemed useless to his way of thinking. I am sure he had been hammered by his father in similar discussions. My dad had wanted to be an actor. Instead he became a charismatic physician.

Through the years, I have often questioned it myself. "What in the world was I thinking getting a liberal arts degree?" My thinking in those moments of doubt was, "Maybe a degree in business or advertising would've gotten me further in my career." I don't believe that thinking is the correct line of thought on the matter.

Here's what you either learn or don't learn at college: the passion for learning something new and the ability to recognize that passion and follow it along to some conclusion. This is different from the "follow your bliss" self-help kind of following. This follow is about YOUR PASSION. In college you finally have the ability to follow the ideas, philosophies, and (potentially) career path that will set the next 30+ years of your future working-life in motion.

In Thomas Moore's *Care of the Soul*, he talks about listening to where your heart gets its greatest excitement. When you talk to others, what topics and ideas really get your blood boiling? Perhaps that is where your soul will be most satisfied.

So I studied Creative Writing at a university with no real idea of what I wanted to do for a living. I wanted to be a writer. I still want to be a writer. And in the last 25+ years since graduating, I have done a good bit of writing. And here's the kicker, I am a writer, simply by the act of writing. There is a difference between being a writer and making a living as a writer. But here's where the new economy gets interesting.

Advertising and marketing have always been a place where writers and creatives could make a living, regardless of their degree path. And in fact, this is where I have spent the bulk of the last quarter of a century. It's not exactly the writing I was thinking of when I started attending Texas State University's MFA program while working at an ad agency. However, I was lucky. I grew a real shine to Tom Grimes, who still teaches there (and was director of the MFA program from 1996 to 2015). Back then Tom was just a damn good professor and semi-successful writer. It was in his class that I really began to feel a pain between what I was doing for a living and what I wanted to be doing. I wanted to be a full-time student, just like 90% of my classmates. I wanted to go to poetry readings, do small press publishing, and most of all I wanted the supportive environment to write.

As I mentioned before, Tom took me out for a beer at a local pub in San Marcos. Here's what he said.

"You are making a good living doing what you do well. These kids in the MFA program will be lucky to find employment when they graduate. Even the students graduating from the Iowa Writer's Workshop are most likely to not find jobs as teachers or writers. It's a tough market. If you want to be a writer, write. Make a living however you can, and then write."

At the beginning of the next semester at Texas State I was enrolled in my first non-creative writing class. A survey class of early English writers. During that first class, when we were learning what books we would be reading in the class and what our "assignments" would look like, it became clear to me that I was done. I dropped out of the MFA program after completing only the creative sequence. I did not ever want to write another academic literary report.

I am still working in marketing. Today it is 90% online. And social media have brought back the craft of writing as a very valuable tool. So now I do write for a living. Not quite the novel/poem/screenplay idea that I had 25 years ago, but still creative and still about words and expression.

And after several years of writing uber.la, almost daily, I have in some aspects become a writer. I balk against being called a blogger. But I guess that's what I am. And if that's what I am, then that's what Seth Godin and Malcom Gladwell are, too. And the answer for me is this: I learned how to use words. I kept my day job. And continued to work my word craft as I could.

In my highest ambition, I am sure I will publish a novel or two, at least a few tech books, and perhaps a screenplay. I would like to be seen, eventually, as a writer. That is my dream and my ambition. I am still pushing towards that idea every day.

And every day I am also working out how to pay my bills. Today I am about 80% of the way there. I am actually doing something I love, as I believe in the power of communication and social media to change the world. I see it changing business, and I am part of that change.

If I were to still have my dad today, I would tell him, "See,

I am doing it. I am writing. I did what I wanted to do, and I am happy."

Find your "know and love" mix in "do for money" and never give up the "ambition and dreams." That's what college is for. Find the formula that works for you.

The Career Path Template

"The point is, in the big picture, no one is going to look after your career for you, but you."
– Erin Malone on Boxes and Arrows: http://boxesandarrows.com/planning-your-future/

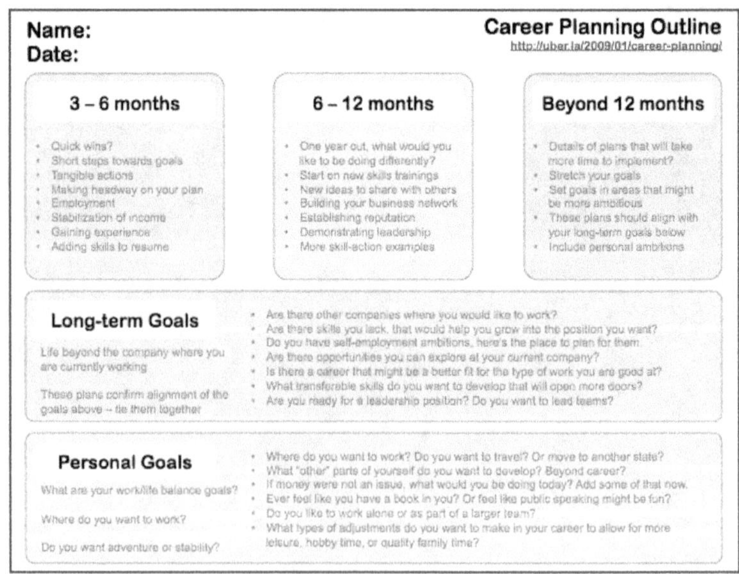

Available for download: from Uber.la

The Career Planning Template:

Your Name

Today's Date

This is important as you reflect back on this document. This will become a touchstone for your growth and a reminder of who you were as you look back at what was important to you in this point in time.

3–6 Months

Start small.

Think about short-term goals that are easily achieved but will also help move you towards the longer-term goals.

Include some tangible goals (e.g., ship a product that I acted as lead designer for).

6–12 Months

Start thinking bigger here—this is planning for a year out.

What new skills do you want to learn?

What new ideas do you want to share with others?

What changes do you want to make? Put them down here along with the steps needed to take to make them happen.

Beyond 12 Months

Capture specific plans that you know may take more than a year to get to or accomplish. Working on a book may take years to come to fruition with an actual proposal in hand and a potential publisher.

Be realistic but not afraid to reach. Visualize success in areas you may have little control over. Don't be afraid to write down a desired goal that may be a stretch.

Long-Term Goals

This is the area to think out for the next 3–5 years, including life beyond the company or situation you are currently in. This goal reminds you what you want to do and that you need to make certain decisions and changes in order to make it happen. If you decide at a later time that you don't really want to do this, you should remove it off the plan.

Opportunities to Explore at Your Company

List all the training and coaching opportunities relevant and currently available at your company.

Note relationships that need to be cultivated at your company in order to meet success.

Note: This obviously may not apply if you are an independent consultant. Think about other opportunities that might be available through professional associations and networking instead.

Skills to Develop

Project what skills you need to develop to reach the goals you listed in the first part of this exercise.

What other skills do you need, besides the ones you have now, to attain your goal? This may include things such as confidence and effectiveness—along with ideas on how to master these more intangible skills. Over the next few years, you may purposely put yourself into situations to gain confidence, for instance. Think about starting slow and building on your successes. In addition, list skills of associated/allied roles that you would like to learn to become more well-rounded and effective.

What I Care About in a Work Environment

This may seem frivolous or not important to the task at hand, but it serves to remind you of the values you need to share with the company (or industry) you work for. As you grow or the company changes, this can help guide you when you need to make a change.

Personal Goals

Don't forget the personal goals that you need to weave into your life. It never hurts to write these down as a reminder of work/life balance and of the things that are really important to you as a person.

Note: Adapted from Erin Malone, *Planning Your Future,* 2004, Boxes and Arrows:

http://boxesandarrows.com/planning-your-future/

Bibliography

Atchity, Kenneth John. (2013). *Write Time: Guide to the Creative Process, From Vision Through Revision—and Beyond.* New York, NY: Norton.

Cameron, Julia. (2016). *The Artist's Way: A Spiritual Path to Higher Creativity: 25th Anniversary Edition.* New York, NY: Penguin Random House.

Cameron, Julia. (2018). *Julia Cameron Live/The Artist's Way.* http://juliacameronlive.com/basic-tools/morning-pages/

Foo Fighters Sonic Highways [HBO TV show]. https://www.hbo.com/foo-fighters-sonic-highways

Goldberg, Natalie. (2018). *Writing Down the Bones: Freeing the Writer Within.*
http://nataliegoldberg.com/books/writing-down-the-bones/

Goldberg, Natalie. (2018). *Writing Down the Bones: Freeing the Writer Within* (Rev. ed.). Boston, MA: Shambhala.

Joyce, James. (1916). *A Portrait of the Artist as a Young Man.* New York, NY: Huebsch.

Kramer, Peter D. (2005). *Against Depression.* New York, NY: Penguin.

MacKenzie, Gordon. (1998). *Orbiting the Giant Hairball: A Corporate Fool's Guide to Surviving with Grace.* New York, NY: Viking.

Malone, Erin. (2004, February 26). *Planning Your Future.* http://boxesandarrows.com/planning-your-future/

Moore, Thomas. (1998). *Care of the Soul: How to Add Depth and Meaning to Your Everyday Life.* New York, NY: Harper-Collins.

Pressfield, Steven. (2002). *The War of Art: Break Through the Blocks and Win Your Inner Creative Battles.* Black Irish Books. https://stevenpressfield.com

Rilke, Rainer Maria. (1929). *Letters to a Young Poet.*

Webb, Jimmy. (1998). *Tunesmith: Inside the Art of Songwriting.* New York, NY: Hyperion.